A Season With The Carmarthenshire Hunt

The 2015-16 Season

Chris Harte

Sports History Publishing

Sports History Publishing

First published in 2016

**by Sports History Publishing in conjunction with
the Carmarthenshire Hunt**

ISBN : 978-1-898010-08-1

Editor : Susan Lewis

Consultant Editor : Lizzie Mead

Front Cover : Michelle Lester

Back Cover : Miranda Bowen

Contact : chrismedia47@yahoo.co.uk

Printed and bound in Wales

CHAPTERS

Recent Books by the Author include

Old Gold (2013)
Watching Brief (2010)
Recollections of a Sportswriter (2009)
The History of Australian Cricket (2008)
Rugby Clubs and Grounds (2005)
English Rugby Clubs (2004)
Britain's Rugby Grounds (2003)
Australian Cricket History (2003)
Reminiscences of a Sportswriter (2002)
Menston Actually (2001)
Sports Books in Britain (2000)
Ramblings of a Sportswriter (1999)
A Year in the Sporting Pressbox (1998)
The Twickenham Papers (1997)
A Sportswriter's Year (1997)
Sporting Heritage (1996)
One Day in Leicester (1995)
A History of Australian Cricket (1993)
Cricket Indulgence (1991)
History of South Australian Cricket (1990)
South African International Cricket (1989)
Two Tours and Pollock (1988)
Seven Tests (1987)
Australians in South Africa (1987)
Cricket Safari (1986)
Australian Cricket Journal (1985)
Cricket Rebels (1985)
The History of the Sheffield Shield (1984)
The Fight for the Ashes (1983)
Cathedral End (1979)

In Preparation

A History and Bibliography of *Baily's Magazine of Sports and Pastimes, 1860-1926*
(to be published in 2017)

A Monograph of the Principal Writers in
Baily's Magazine of Sports and Pastimes, 1860-1926
(to be published in 2018)

Hunting in Carmarthenshire
(to be published in 2019)

INTRODUCTION

The 177th year of a formal Hunt Club in Carmarthenshire started on a bright but windy day in October 2015. The venue was Laugharne, a place more associated in the mind with the poet Dylan Thomas rather than rows upon rows of horse boxes.

The base for the day was the *Fountain Inn*, a public house facing The Grist, the small town's equivalent of a market square. Many years ago in a book titled *Inns of Sport* the author wrote: 'The day the pub dies, Britain dies; for in the pub you will find the heart of the country.'

He was, of course, completely right for sport is as much a part of the British character as the inn is of British life. They make the perfect union, being complementary to each other as good partners should be. Can you imagine a better place for a meet of foxhounds than *The Fox and Hounds*? Or, in this instance, the *Fountain Inn*.

Before the first meet took place a Horse, Pony & Dog Show had been organised at Bragty Farm, near Bancyfelin. It took place on a lovely day in early September and the field set aside for horseboxes was virtually full. Organised by Dai Jones the event attracted numerous entries and went like clockwork.

Seven weeks later came the Laugharne meet with sixty-five horses and riders gathering in the town's car-park. The day was fine which attracted quite a number of followers and spectators. A week later the meet started from Bancyfelin in what turned out to be the driest day for some time. Hermon, on the last day of October, saw damp conditions underfoot but Roger and Linda were perfect hosts.

The weather started to deteriorate for the meet at Llangynin with the evening's entertainment based in Llanboidy. Jacqui Kedward was the organiser for what was named 'The Carmarthenshire Hunt Club's Llanboidy Farmers' Ball.'

Mid-November and the meet at Cynwyl Elfed was conducted in a howling gale. Before the start many gathered inside the cosy Blue Bell Inn to have a few heart-warming drinks before starting off. The limited number of photographs from the day show just how bad the conditions became.

The following Saturday it was a trip up into the hills to gather at Blaenwaun. The inside of the Lamb Inn was inviting although the bad weather had relented a bit. The turnout was good and the day turned out to be the best for some time.

The last meet in November saw many horseboxes line the main street in Llandyfaelog. The initial gathering was at the Red Lion where Edwin Atkinson was briefing Acting-Master Dai Jones on the trail the dogs could take through his land and those of his neighbours.

Incredibly strong winds greeted the riders the following week at Llanfyrnach. The turnout was initially low but as time drew on so more people walked into the Pantyblaidd Inn in search of some warmth. There was a little difficulty in getting horses from their boxes but willing hands held doors open while the animals disembarked.

The Smiths Arms in Llangyndeyrn was not only the base for the mid-month meet but also the host for the evening's Christmas Dinner. Over fifty riders took part in the afternoon's event although for much of the time the rain poured down incessantly. The dinner proved to be a hugely enjoyable occasion with the younger riders having a long table all to themselves while the adults gathered in their various groups.

The Saturday before Christmas saw the Farmers Arms at Llanybri host the Hunt. It had been a bit of a struggle to get to the village as some roads were impassable due to flooding. Attendance was low but that was to be expected for the time of year and the adverse conditions.

Our friend Geoff kindly allowed the first midweek meet of the season to gather at his farm in Meinciau. The weather was atrocious as can be seen by the few photographs which were taken.

The Boxing Day meet at the Fountain Inn in Meidrim was a pleasure to attend. The rain had stopped and by mid-morning drinkers were overflowing into the Inn's front yard. Supporters were gathering in their hundreds while the line of horseboxes trailed way back up the Drefach Road. The atmosphere was one of goodwill and camaraderie with the bar doing a roaring trade. Later on in the day the returning riders were treated to hot cawl as well as a good selection of food. It is places like the Fountain Inn which make you realise that pubs and hunts go hand in glove.

The Tuesday after Christmas saw the Hunt meet at Rhodri's farm in Pontantwn. His welcome hot brew was taken up by most people which included visitors from The Vale of Clettwr Hunt. There was still an awful lot of mud around and to see the state of some riders' clothing at the end of the day showed exactly how bad things had been.

So that finished the year 2015 for the Hunt. They were now halfway through the season which, in all honesty, had been very badly affected by the wind, rain and excessive wintry conditions.

The previous few months did, however, produce some amusing incidents some of which have been captured either by camera or by 'phone. They are interspersed among the pages of this book.

New Year's Day stayed mainly dry for the Hunt's big event. The traditional meet outside the Guildhall in the centre of Carmarthen. What no one expected was such an enormous turnout of riders and supporters. Over eighty-five horses paraded their way past the gathered throng, estimated by the police on duty to have been about four hundred in Guildhall Square with another three hundred lining adjoining streets.

The rousing cheers which greeted Hunt Master Martin Walters and huntsman Owain Fisher came from those who understood the benefits the Hunt has upon the community. Many in the crowd were farming people whose patronage has always been appreciated by the Hunt. Drinks were served to the riders with the compliments of the owners of town public houses who use this opportunity to show their strong support.

Later in the day many of the riders returned to the Boar's Head Hotel to warm themselves and to partake of the hospitality on offer. The following night the Hunt started their New Year party at the hotel before moving on to the Gremlin Club. A few photographs of these events are on page forty-eight.

Eight days later the meet was based at the Lamb Inn in Llanboidy, the village where Walter Powell founded the Hunt in 1839. Originally called the Maesgwynne Foxhounds the Hunt was locally better known by the name Carmarthen Hounds whereas from 1843 newspapers referred to it as Powell's Hounds. Although the day was damp many of the villagers turned out to give the Hunt their support.

A week later and the incessant rain had turned much of the lower part of Llansteffan into a quagmire. Riders were muddied before they started the day. Early drinks were taken in the newly renovated Sticks Hotel before the horn was blown and the Hunt trotted off with the cheers of the crowd ringing in their ears.

Unfortunately around twenty-four misguided young men, all wearing woollen balaclavas, had been bussed in from some distance (mainly Bristol) in order to try and cause trouble. Their cowardly and vulgar abuse, especially towards the younger riders, continued for most of the day. They also repeatedly blew a horn which attracted the hounds on to the main Llansteffan road where injuries occurred. All this from alleged animal lovers.

Fortunately the Hunt were able to enjoy the following Saturday's meet which took place at Trelech. The landlord of the Beca Inn was the host and his warm rooms and kind hospitality meant a lot to those present. The cold blustery wind was the order of the day and riders wrapped up well for their amble around the countryside.

The end of January saw the Hunt at Llanglydwen. This time it was the warmth of The Bont which was so welcome. Numbers were down for various reasons but that did not stop two Land Rovers full of balaclava wearing students from the University of the West of England making a nuisance of themselves.

Led by a professional protestor from Newport the students (who were not only paid £30 each for the day but also were given packed lunches) ran around like lost children, eventually giving some of the hounds a hug before departing. Because of their stupidity and the laying of a false scent three hounds were lost and not found until late the following day.

In the evening Anthony James had organised a Tippet Evening at the Black Lion Hotel in St.Clears. The place was crowded; friends had an pleasant evening; the sponsors were generous; competition was intense and the winners enjoyed their success. It was a prelude to the following week's Hunt Ball.

A few days later the Annual General Meeting was held at the Boar's Head Hotel. Everything went smoothly helped mainly by Rhodri Wilkin's excellent six page breakdown of the Hunt Club's finances. Membership had shown another upward turn and future predictions looked rosy.

The first meet of February started from the Prince of Wales in Porthyrhyd. The weather was as atrocious as ever but this did not stop a large number of members and supporters from attending. Visitors came from along the M4 corridor which added to the forty or so local horses and riders. Vashti Hasdell had arranged for a pre-Hunt breakfast to be available so there was no excuse for hunger pangs during the day.

The evening saw the Hunt Ball take place at the Ivy Bush Royal Hotel in Carmarthen. Organised by Amanda Sloyan the whole event went off with military precision. As always the meal was excellent and the entertainment was of top quality. A custom of the Hunt is to make awards for the season and these were duly given to Anthony James, Daniel George, Oli Farrier and Asher Jenkins.

A week later it was the short trip north of Carmarthen to the Plough & Harrow Inn at Trevaughan. This pub has been welcoming the Hunt for well over a century and is renowned for its support of country people and their ways. Although damp underfoot the rain held off and the Hunt riders were able to move a little faster than normal. However, this did not stop quite a number of them having their names entered in the 'tumbler's book.'

The following Tuesday, with Spring in the air, a children's meet took place at Talog. In this part of the county the valleys are steep and tracks have to be followed without deviation. But that did not stop the youngsters having a splendid day, one which was slightly soured by the theft of some money from one of the Hunt's vehicles parked in the Bethania Chapel car-park.

For the third Saturday of February the meet had been arranged at the coastal resort of Pendine. The rain and wind howled in from the sea and the warmth of the Green Bridge Inn was very welcome. Even so, some thirty-five brave souls faced the elements on their horses while most of the foot-followers watched from their vehicles.

About this time a year ago the Hunt had welcomed visitors from the Home Counties. The Kimblewick Hunt, which had been formed in 2002, came for a joint-meet. They took the title in 2010 as the kennels were based in the village of the same name which is situated near to Aylesbury. Previously they were old hunts known as the Garth, South Berkshire, the Old Berkeley, South Oxfordshire, Hertfordshire and Vale of Aylesbury; all of whom had amalgamated over the years. The history of these hunts form the basis of the story of fox-hunting.

Now it was the Carmarthenshire Hunt's turn to visit the huge area covered by the Kimblewick. The country covered parts of Bedfordshire, Berkshire, Buckinghamshire, Hampshire, Hertfordshire and Oxfordshire; sixty-five miles north to south and forty miles east to west. The terrain varied widely: from woodland to heath; from grass to plough with jumpable hedges, ditches and rail fences.

The meet took place at Poors Farm in Hailey which bordered onto the northern edge of the Chiltern Hills. There were a few sore heads early on as the previous evening had been spent in The Swan at Great Kimble. With the sun shining on the Oxfordshire countryside some fifty horses took off for what became a memorable day for the visitors.

In the evening the Kimblewick had their annual Hunt Ball. It was held at Kingston House, a stone's throw from the nearby motorway, and from the many photos placed on social media it was clear that the hunting fraternity knows how to enjoy themselves.

The penultimate hunt of the season was held on the first Saturday in March at Gellywen on a farm overlooking the Cynis Valley. Mary, our sociable hostess, had food and drink awaiting the day's visitors.

For once the bad weather held off and although there was a biting northerly wind the sky was blue: a welcome change from the recent past. The day showed that spring was around the corner as can be observed in the photographs which were taken.

The final meet was held to the east of Llangynin where Bill and Emma were the hosts. The day was perfect and nearly seventy horses started out. All was going well until Kirsty had a tumble which (as we found out later) resulted in her breaking two vertebrae at the top of her spine.

With the hunt season over it was time to look at the organisation of the Point-to-Point meeting which, as usual, would be held over the course at Lydstep. This joint venture with the Tivyside Hunt needed plenty of arranging with the Monday evening meetings at the Boars Head each lasting for quite some time.

By now it was known that huntsman Owain Fisher and his partner, Asher Jenkins, would be leaving the area. Owain was going to take up a similar position with the Ross Harriers. This was yet another excuse for the Hunt to organise a party, which took place in the Gremlin Club, and make presentations to the departing couple.

The day of the Lydstep meeting was fine but with a cold, blustery wind. With help from members of both Hunts as well as from the South Pembrokeshire the course was perfect for a day's racing. Marquees, gazebos, children's entertainments and hot food vehicles were all stocked and ready for the start.

The Hunt Members, Subscribers & Farmers Race had more than a passing interest for Carmarthenshire followers as Ben Jones and Bobby Thomas were both involved. Later in the day two of the Hunt's younger members, Sarah Evans and Hannah Jones, rode in the First Pony Race. The meeting went like clockwork, in many ways due to the fine organisation by Annette Kemp. Eighty helpers were named in the Race Card but quite a few more gave of their time.

This left only the Hound, Terrier, Lurcher and Whippet Show which is organised on an annual basis by Anthony James. Held at the Pantyathro Welsh Equitation Centre, which is situated south of Llangain, the day went off perfectly. The spring weather was excellent and entries were attracted from far and wide.

So that was it for the 2015-16 season. Membership is on the rise; participation is on a good level. The Hunt continues to be as popular as ever and long may it be so.

In conclusion it must be noted that quite a number of the photographs in this book were taken by Hunt members. They kindly co-operated with my requests during the season the results of which are seen on the following pages.

I hope you all enjoy the memories.

Braemar House
Carmarthen   July 2016

Record numbers in the saddle for show

THE Annual Carmarthenshire Horse and Pony Show was held at Bragty Farm in Bancyfelin last weekend.

Organised by the Carmarthenshire Hunt Club, there were a record number of entries for the thirty-six classes being judged during the day.

For the second successive year the supreme champion at the show was awarded to Catrin Brunt of Llangunnor who was riding her horse Cassie. Catrin, and attends Bro Myrddin School..

In the Hunters' Class the overall Champion was Tim Rees of Meidrim on Smalland Shoreline with the Reserve Champion going to Owen Thomas of Laugharne.

The Working Hunter and Ponies Class went to Catrin Brunt with the Reserve Champion awarded to Celyn Tate of Burry Port on Franco. In the Showing Classes the

SECOND TIME: Supreme Champion Catrin Brunt receiving the cup from Jo Shewry.

Champion In-Hand was Tracy Jones of Bancyffordd riding Grey Court with Eleanor Phillips of Llangynog on Mel being Reserve Champion. The show-jumping event was won by Newcastle Emlyn's Sofia Cynwyl, on Mabli.

Ring 5.
Unaffiliated Show Jumping (10am)
(Juniors and Seniors to jump in same class – Split for jump-off)
J1. Minimus – Lead Rein Permitted (Max 1'6")
J2. Junior / Seniors Beginners (Max 1'9")
J3. Junior / Senior Novice Max (2'3")
J4. Pairs Any Combination (1st Rider 2'3" / 2nd Rider 2'6") (£6 Entry)
J5. Scurry – (Set course to be jumped in fastest time) Max 2' 6"
J6. Junior / Senior Intermediate (2'6") Not to have won open Jumping class
J7. Junior / Senior Mini Open (2'9")
J8. Junior / Senior Open (3')
J9. Treble Combination Chase Me Charlie (First Round 2')
(£25 Winner Take All)

Rules & Show Conditions

- The Committee and Land Owner cannot be held responsible for any loss, damage, injury, or illness to horse, owner, rider, handler, or any other spectator or property whatsoever; from accidents or any other cause
- No entries will be accepted without the correct fee
- No horse or pony to be left unattended
- All mounted persons must wear a riding hat with harness fastened
- All dogs must be kept on leads at all times
- All ridden horses and ponies must be 4 years old or over
- Any persons found breaking any rules will be expelled from the showground
- Any exhibitor lodging a protest/complaint must first deposit £10 with the Secretary, which will be forfeited to the fund if the complaint is not upheld. All complaints must be lodged before the end of the show.
- The decision of the judges in all competitions, and that of the dispute committee in cases of complaints, will be final and without further appeal.
- The committee reserve the right to amend, cancel or change classes at their discretion

CARMARTHENSHIRE HUNT
Annual Horse, Pony, & Dog Show
Including Unaffiliated Show Jumping and Gymkhana
At
BRAGTY FARM, BANCYFELIN.
(By Kind permission of Mr Hansard Jones)
On
SUNDAY 7th SEPTEMBER 2014.
To Start at 9.30am.

Food and Refreshments Available on Showground

Entry Fee in All Classes, Unless Otherwise Stated –
CHC Members - £3.50 Pre Show (£4 On Day)
Non-Members - £4 Pre Show (£5 On Day)
£2 per person to Cover First Aid Fee.

Entries Before The Day To –
Dai Jones
Pengerddi
Glangwili
Carmarthen
SA32 7HR
07736 553011

(Cheques Made Payable To – Carmarthenshire Hunt)

The Committee would like to thank all sponsors, judges, stewards, helpers and competitors for their continued support.

Supreme Champion – To Be Judged By Mr Hansard Jones

Ring 1.
Hunters (Not to Start Before 11am)
1. Novice Hunter, over 14.2hh, Not to have won 1st prize
2. Open Hunter – exceeding 15.2hh
3. Small Hunter – Exceeding 14.2hh but not Exceeding 15.2hh
4. Riding Cob
5. Riding Horse – Exceeding 14.2hh
6. Racehorse to Riding Horse
7. Brood Mare & Foal (In-Hand)
8. Hunter Yearling or two year old (In-Hand)
9. Hunter 3 yr old
10. Championship (Classes 1 – 9)

Ring 2
Working Hunter and Ponies (9.30am)
11. Novice Working Hunter, not to have won a 1st prize. Max 2'6"
12. Racehorse to Riding Horse, max height 2'6" Max 6 Fences.
13. Open Working Hunter
Not to start before 11am
14. Mountain and Moorland WHP – Small Breeds
15. Mountain and moorland WHP – Large Breeds
16. Cradle Stakes
17. Nursery Stakes
18. Mixed Height Novice
19. 13hh Open
20. 14hh Open
21. 15hh Open
22. Intermediate
23. Championship (Classes 11 – 22)

Dog Show
Classes for –
Coolest Pup; Loveliest Lady; Best Mini Miss; Fantastic Fella; Dinky Boy; Golden Oldie; Awesome Eyes; Best Junior Handler; Cute Crossbreed; Dog Judge would like to take home; Waggiest Tail & Best in Show.

Ring 3
Showing Classes (9.30am)
1. Open In-hand Condition and Turnout
2. Open Ridden Condition and Turnout
3. Best In-Hand Coloured Horse or Pony
4. Best Ridden Coloured Horse or Pony
5. Best In-Hand Veteran Horse and Pony, 16yrs and over
6. Best Ridden Veteran Horse and Pony, 16yrs and over
7. Best In-Hand Pure or Part Bred Arab
8. Best Ridden Pure or Part-Bred Arab
9. Best In-Hand Welsh
10. Best Ridden Welsh
11. Best In-Hand Welsh Part Bred
12. Best Ridden Welsh Part Bred
13. Best In-Hand Palomino
14. Best Ridden Palomino
15. Best Lead-Rein Pony (Rider 9yrs Under)
16. Best First Ridden Pony (Rider 11yrs Under)
17. Best Junior Handler (Under 16)
18. Best Junior Rider (Under 16)
19. Best In-Hand Shetland, Any Age
20. Best Ridden Shetland, Over 4yrs
21. Best Ridden Trekking Horse or Pony
22. Best Fancy Dress
23. Championship – In-Hand and Ridden

Ring 4.
Clear Round Jumping – 9.30am Until 3pm.
Jumps Any Height – Entry Fee £2 With Rosette, £1 Without –

Gymkhana – Start 3pm. – Entry Fee £1 per Class
Bending; One up Polo; Walk, Trot Canter; Other Pony Club Games
Class 1 – Lead Rein (Not to be entered in other Classes)
Class 2 – 12 & Under
Class 3 – Open

Carmarthen Hunt
Perpetual Challenge Trophy
In Memory Of
Arthur Shewry

Journal
country life farming

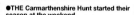

●THE Carmarthenshire Hunt started their season at the weekend.

The Hunt held their first meeting in Laugharne, an area perfect for riding.

There were 64 mounted riders who started from the park at the base of Laugharne Castle with others joining later.

The annual invitation from Laugharne Corporation and the ready agreement of local farmers for the Hunt to ride on their land are always appreciated by Hunt members.

To add to the colourful day over three hundred foot followers and supporters turned out to give their cheers to Huntsman Owain Fisher as he led the pack.

Unfortunately, the Master, Martin Walters was recovering from a riding accident which meant that former Master, Dai Jones took on the role.

The popularity of the Carmarthenshire can be shown by its ever rising list of members which now exceeds well over four figures.

Community

Hunt season starts with Laugharne meeting

THE CARMARTHENSHIRE HUNT began their season . on Saturday (Oct 17) with a meeting at Laugharne.

Although Laugharne is better-known for its relationship with the poet Dylan Thomas, the area is also perfect for riding, as the many riders who turned up could testify.

A representative of the Hunt told The Herald that a 'splendid day' was had by all. There were initially 64 mounted riders who started from the park at the base of Laugharne Castle, while may other riders joined in later.

The annual invitation from Laugharne Corporation and the ready agreement of local farmers for the Hunt to ride on their land are always appreciated by Hunt members.

To add to the colourful day over three hundred foot-followers and supporters turned out to give their cheers to Huntsman Owain Fisher as he led the pack. Unfortunately, the Master, Martin Walters was recovering from a riding accident which meant that former Master, Dai Jones took on the role.

The popularity of the Carmarthenshire can be shown by its ever rising list of members which now exceeds well over four figures.

LLANGYNIN

LLANBOIDY FARMERS' BALL

LAMB INN, BLAENWAUN

PANT-Y-BLAIDD INN, LLANFYRNACH

SMITHS ARMS, CHRISTMAS DINNER

FARMERS ARMS, LLANYBRI

FOR FAST RIDERS
WE HAVE FAST HORSES,
FOR SLOW RIDERS
WE HAVE SLOW HORSES.
FOR THOSE WHO HAVE NEVER
RIDDEN,
WE HAVE HORSES THAT
HAVE NEVER BEEN RIDDEN.

G. STONE.

FOUNTAIN INN, MEIDRIM

FOUNTAIN INN, MEIDRIM

FOUNTAIN INN, MEIDRIM

FOUNTAIN INN, MEIDRIM

FOUNTAIN INN, MEIDRIM

SOME END OF YEAR PICTURES

TWO OLD HUNT CHRISTMAS CARDS

47

THE BELATED NEW YEAR'S PARTY

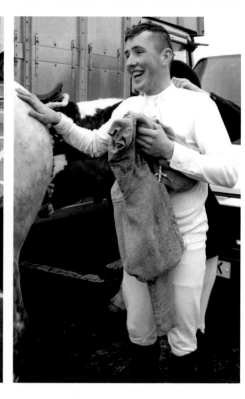

Support for hunting within the law

DEAR SIR,

I have found myself completely frustrated over recent weeks by the propaganda being put out by those who are against any sort of hunting with hounds.

There is, in fact, overwhelming support for hunting (within the law) as demonstrated on New Year's Day in Carmarthen town centre. Some five hundred local people turned out by Guildhall with adjoining streets crammed with cheering spectators.

A recent online poll about hunting seems to have been hijacked by keyboard warriors who can hit a yes or no button from any part of the world. The figures given out from this poll were the type expected from an election in one of the world's dictatorships.

The proof of the pudding about the support for hunting came on our own doorstep when the sheer numbers of those turning up at the Boxing Day and New Year's Day hunt was calculated to be nearly one thousand Carmarthenshire residents.

Name and address supplied

LAMB INN, LLANBOIDY

OKAY, THIS TIME MAKE A FUNNY FACE

THE BONT, LLANGLYDWEN

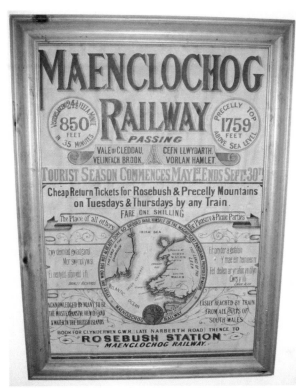

ANNUAL GENERAL MEETING

PRINCE OF WALES, PORTHYRHYD

PRINCE OF WALES, PORTHYRHYD

HUNT BALL, CARMARTHEN

HUNT BALL, CARMARTHEN

PLOUGH & HARROW INN, TREVAUGHAN

BETHANIA CHAPEL, TALOG

GELLYWEN

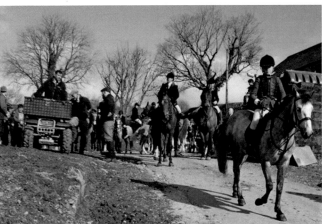

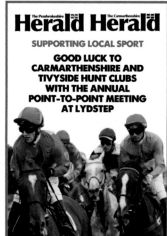

The Pembrokeshire **Herald** The Carmarthenshire **Herald**

SUPPORTING LOCAL SPORT

**GOOD LUCK TO
CARMARTHENSHIRE AND
TIVYSIDE HUNT CLUBS
WITH THE ANNUAL
POINT-TO-POINT MEETING
AT LYDSTEP**

Carmarthenshire Hunt Hound, Terrier, Lurcher & Whippet Show

Saturday 7th May 2016
at
Pantyathro
Welsh Equitation Centre
Llansteffan, Carmarthen, SA33 5AJ

Bar & BBQ

Adult Admission - £2.00   Children - Free

The Hunting Act
was never about
animal welfare, it is
a prejudice act
against the people of
the countryside.

Repeal the Hunting Act

of the people that call in to
this column.

To all you hunters who
kill animals for food,
shame on you; you ought
to go to the store and buy
the meat that was made
there, where no animals
were harmed.

I am calling in regard to
the Speakout. I am an avid